My First Japanese Kanji Book

Learning kanji the fun and easy way!

はじめての漢字の本

Written by Anna Sato and Eriko Sato
Illustrated by Anna Sato

TUTTLE PUBLISHING

Tokyo • Rutland, Vermont • Singapore

To Anna's late grandfather, Yoshio Sato

Acknowledgments

The authors are grateful to Anna's grandfather, the late Yoshio Sato, and her grandmother, Etsuko Sato, in Japan, as well as the students of the Pre-College Japanese Program at the State University of New York at Stony Brook, for inspiring them to write this book for English/Japanese bilingual children and for others interested in learning basic kanji in context. Being able to talk with one's grandparents and relatives to express love and share culture and tradition is a special life-time treasure to be cherished by one's entire family, and ultimately becomes a life-time strength.

The creation of this book involved an enjoyable mother-daughter collaboration through language teaching and learning. Special thanks to Anna's cousin, Kota Motonaga, and his parents, Yoshinori and Yumiko Motonaga, for their continued and selfless help. The authors are also grateful to Anna's art teacher, June Adinolfi, for enthusiastically and effectively guiding her to create all 36 illustrations in this book over the past four years, and to Tuttle's editors, Bob Graham and Sandra Korinchak, and the designer, Sook Fan Loh, for their professionalism, dedication, and kindness. Last but not least, special heartfelt thanks to Yimei Zhu, Anna's father and Eriko's husband, for his never-ending support and for being excited about this book with us.

Published by Tuttle Publishing, an imprint of Periplus Editions (HK) Ltd., with editorial offices at 364 Innovation Drive, North Clarendon, Vermont 05759 U.S.A.

Copyright © 2009 by Periplus Editions (HK) Ltd.

Library of Congress Cataloging-in-Publication Data

Sato, Anna.
  My first Japanese Kanji book : learn Kanji the fun and easy way! / written by Anna Sato and Eriko Sato ; illustrated by Anna Sato.
    p. cm.
  ISBN 978-4-8053-1037-3 (alk. paper)
1. Chinese characters--Japan. 2. Japanese language--Orthography and spelling. I. Sato, Eriko, 1962- II. Title.
  PL528.S37 2009
  495.6'82421--dc22
                                       2008055783

First edition
13 12 11 10 09   10 9 8 7 6 5 4 3 2 1

Distributed by:

North America, Latin America & Europe
Tuttle Publishing
364 Innovation Drive, North Clarendon,
VT 05759-9436 U.S.A
Tel: 1 (802) 773 8930Fax: 1 (802) 773 6993
info@tuttlepublishing.com
www.tuttlepublishing.com

Japan
Tuttle Publishing
Yaekari Building, 3rd Floor, 5-4-12 Osaki,
Shinagawa-ku, Tokyo 141 0032
Tel: (81) 3 5437-0171; Fax: (81) 3 5437-0755
tuttle-sales@gol.com

Asia-Pacific
Berkeley Books Pte Ltd
61 Tai Seng Avenue #02-12, Singapore 534167
Tel: (65) 6280-3320; Fax: (65) 6280-6290
inquiries@periplus.com.sg
www.periplus.com

ISBN: 978-4-8053-1037-3

Printed in Singapore

CONTENTS

PREFACE

This kanji book introduces 109 kanji characters to Japanese or Japanese-English bilingual children (kindergarten or elementary school) who have already mastered hiragana and katakana, and who want to learn kanji for the first time with culturally rich and age-appropriate poems and illustrations. It includes all the first grade level kanji characters and some second to sixth grade kanji characters. This book can be used as a self-study text, a teaching material by parents or tutors, a supplementary material in overseas Japanese language schools, or a gift book from family, relatives, or friends.

The kanji characters are introduced according to their degree of relevance to children's daily lives as well as according to the degree of complexity of the characters. The information provided for each character (pronunciation, stroke order, usage examples, and English translations) is kept to a minimum so that it will not overwhelm young learners of kanji. There are 36 lessons; each lesson introduces two to four kanji characters and a poem that uses them. The poems reflect children's viewpoints or Japanese parents' childhood memories, and are short and easy to read aloud, memorize, and recite. As they read the poems, children can experience Japanese culture, recognize concepts and values in Japanese society, develop curiosity about nature (animals, landscapes, weather, universe, body, health, life, etc.), and think of their social relationships with family, friends, schoolmates, and teachers. Each poem is accompanied by a friendly illustration to help children understand, enjoy, visualize, and remember it.

Children can study a lesson each day or each week. Furigana (pronunciation guides for kanji characters) and English translations are provided for each of the poems. By reading the poems repeatedly without relying on furigana and translations, children reinforce their acquisition of kanji. In addition, each new kanji is accompanied by stroke-order diagrams, sample vocabulary, and boxes for writing practice. Children may also use the accompanying MP3 audio CD to listen to the poems read in Japanese and in English. It is our hope that children will attain a feeling of accomplishment by completing all the lessons and learning to read the poems with new kanji confidently.

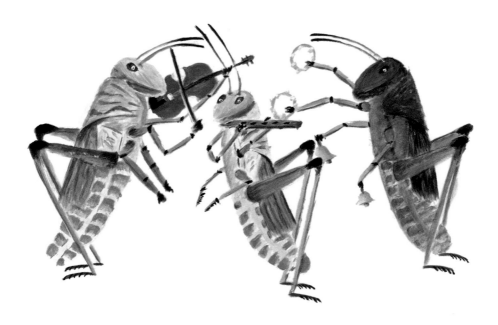

からて Karate (一・二・三)

からての　れんしゅう
Practicing karate;

いち　に　さん
一、二、三。
one, two, three.

からだを　きたえる
Strengthening my body;

いち　に　さん
一、二、三。
one, two, three.

こころも　きたえる
Strengthening my spirit, too;

いち　に　さん
一、二、三。
one, two, three.

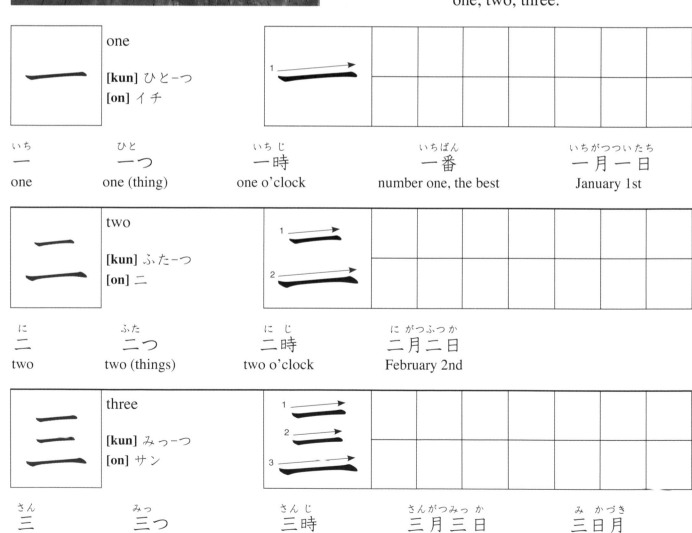

one	
一	[kun] ひと－つ
	[on] イチ

いち　　　　ひと　　　　いちじ　　　　いちばん　　　　いちがつついたち
一　　　　一つ　　　　一時　　　　一番　　　　一月一日
one　　　one (thing)　　one o'clock　　number one, the best　　January 1st

two	
二	[kun] ふた－つ
	[on] ニ

に　　　　ふた　　　　にじ　　　　にがつふつか
二　　　　二つ　　　　二時　　　　二月二日
two　　　two (things)　　two o'clock　　February 2nd

three	
三	[kun] みっ－つ
	[on] サン

さん　　　　みっ　　　　さんじ　　　　さんがつみっか　　　　みかづき
三　　　　三つ　　　　三時　　　　三月三日　　　　三日月
three　　　three (things)　　three o'clock　　March 3rd　　crescent moon

こうえん Park (Playground) (人・子)

きょうは　おてんき。
It's a nice day.

ここは　こうえん。
This is a playground.

あっ、おとこの子が　いる。
Oh, there are boys.

一人、二人、三人。
One, two, three.

だれか　ぼくと　あそんでくれないかな。
I wonder if somebody would play with me.

ゆうきを　だして、「あそぼう」って、
いって　みようかな。
I wonder if I should gather my courage and ask them,
"Can I play with you?"

人

man, person

[kun] ひと
[on] ジン／ニン

あの人
that person

男の人
man

女の人
woman

アメリカ人
American person

日本人
Japanese person

外国人
foreigner

人間
human being

主人
one's own husband

一人、二人、三人、四人、五人
one, two, three, four, five person(s)

子

child

[kun] こ
[on] シ

子ども
child

男の子
boy

女の子
girl

女子学生
female student

おじいちゃんの いなか My Grandpa's Inaka (山・川)

おじいちゃんの　いなかは　くうきが　おいしい。
The air tastes good in my grandpa's inaka (hometown in the countryside).

やま
山が　ある。
There are mountains.

かわ
川も　ある。
There are also rivers.

やま
山に　いって、さんさいを　とる。
We go to the mountain, and pick wild vegetables.

かわ
川に　いって、さかなを　つる。
We go to the river, and fish.

また、なつに　なったら、いきたいな。おじいちゃんの　いなか。
When the summer comes again, I want to go back to my grandpa's inaka.

山　mountain

[kun] やま
[on] サン

ふ じ さん
富士山
Mt. Fuji

さんちょう
山頂
summit

やまのぼ
山登り
mountain climbing

やまぐに
山国
mountainous country

やま だ
山田さん
Mr./Ms./Mrs. Yamada

川　river

[kun] かわ／－がわ
[on]（セン）

かわ
川
river

お がわ
小川
brook, stream

と ね がわ
利根川
the Tone River

がわ
ナイル川
the Nile River

かわぐち
川口さん
Mr./Ms./Mrs. Kawaguchi

お日さまと、お月さま The Sun and the Moon (日・月・明)

お日さまは　ぼくが　そとで　あそんでるとき、
いつも　いっしょに　いてくれる。
When I'm playing outside, the sun is always with me.

お月さまは　おとうさんが　おうちに　かえるとき、
いつも　いっしょに　ついてきてくれる。
When my dad comes home, the moon always comes with him.

お日さまと、お月さまは　いつも　たかい　ところから、
ぼくたちを　みていてくれる。
The sun and the moon always watch over us from high up there.

いつも　たかい　ところから、ぼくたちの　まわりを　明るく　してくれる。
They always brighten the place around us from high up there.

すごいな。
They are amazing!

かみさまみたい。
They are like gods!

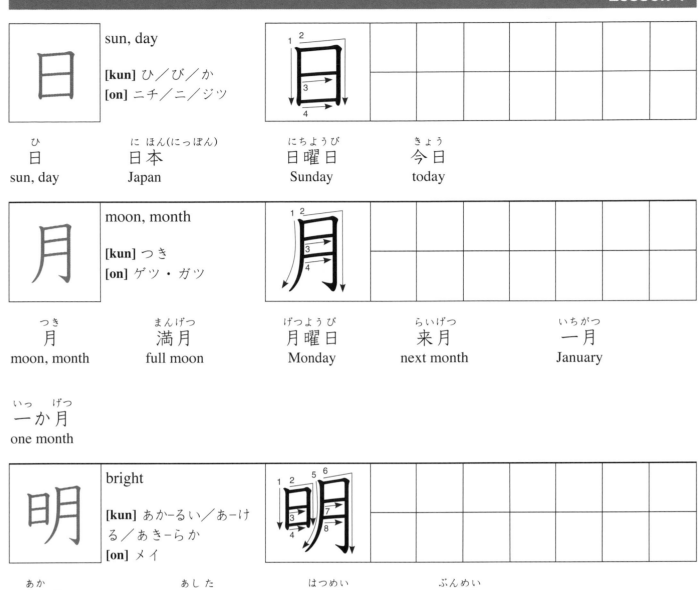

日

sun, day

[kun] ひ／び／か

[on] ニチ／ニ／ジツ

ひ
日
sun, day

に ほん(にっぽん)
日本
Japan

にちようび
日曜日
Sunday

きょう
今日
today

月

moon, month

[kun] つき

[on] ゲツ・ガツ

つき
月
moon, month

まんげつ
満月
full moon

げつようび
月曜日
Monday

らいげつ
来月
next month

いちがつ
一月
January

いっ　げつ
一か月
one month

明

bright

[kun] あかーるい／あーけ
る／あきーらか

[on] メイ

あか
明るい
bright, cheerful

あした
明日
tomorrow

はつめい
発明
invention

ぶんめい
文明
civilization

11

いもうと My Little Sister (目・口・見)

いもうとは　うれしくなると、目が　たれちゃう。
When my little sister becomes happy, her eyes turn into lines slightly slanted down.

いもうとは　おこると、口が　とんがっちゃう。
When my little sister gets mad, her mouth is pursed.

いもうとは　ねると、口も、目も、つむっちゃう。
When my little sister sleeps, both her eyes and mouth close.

いいゆめ　見てね。ななちゃん。
Sweet dreams, Nana-chan.

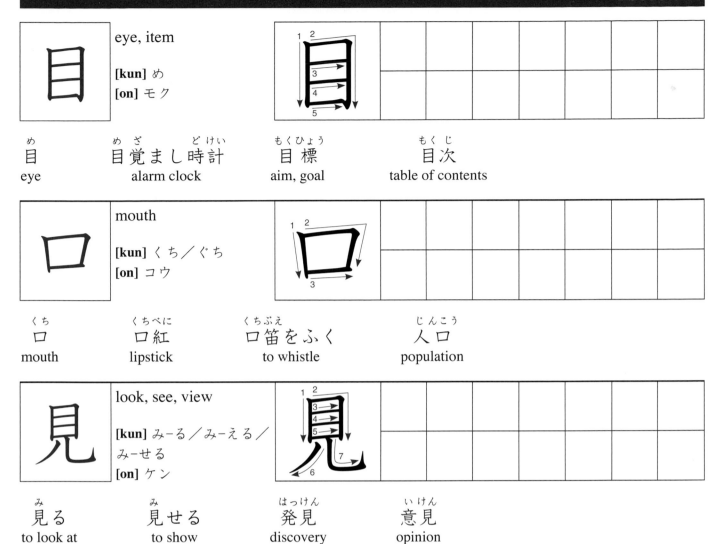

目　eye, item
[kun] め
[on] モク

め
目
eye

めざ　どけい
目覚まし時計
alarm clock

もくひょう
目標
aim, goal

もくじ
目次
table of contents

口　mouth
[kun] くち／ぐち
[on] コウ

くち
口
mouth

くちべに
口紅
lipstick

くちぶえ
口笛をふく
to whistle

じんこう
人口
population

見　look, see, view
[kun] みーる／みーえる／
みーせる
[on] ケン

み
見る
to look at

み
見せる
to show

はっけん
発見
discovery

いけん
意見
opinion

木のあるところ Places with Trees (木・林・森)

林の　なかは　しずかで、すずしくて、きもちいい。
In the woods, it is quiet, cool, and soothing.

かぜが　木と木の　あいだを　すうっと　とおる。
The breeze can pass through the trees.

ぼくも　かけまわる。
I can run through the trees, too.

森の　なかは　いろんな木が　ごちゃごちゃ　している。
The forest is crowded with all sorts of trees.

森の　なかは　えだを　かきわけながら　あるく。
As I walk, I need to slash my way through the forest.

まいごに　なったら、くまさんに　あうかも。
If I get lost, I may encounter Mr. Bear!

tree

[kun] き
[on] モク／ボク

き	もくようび	もくせい	ぼくとう
木	木曜日	木星	木刀
tree, wood	Thursday	Jupiter	wooden sword

wood, grove

[kun] はやし
[on] リン

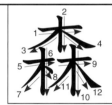

はやし	まつばやし	はやし
林	松林	林さん
woods	pinewood	Mr./Ms./Mrs. Hayashi

森

forest, jungle

[kun] もり
[on] シン

もり	しんりん	もり
森	森林	森さん
forest	woods and forests	Mr./Ms./Mrs. Mori

はな火 Sparklers (火・光・水)

なつの　よるは　はな火を　します。
On a summer night, we play with sparklers.

ちいさい　光が　キラキラ、パチパチ。
Tiny lights sparkle and crackle.

ゆめみたいに　きれい。
Like a dream, it's beautiful.

はな火を　するときは　おとなの人と
しましょう。
When you play with sparklers,
you must do so with adults.

バケツの　水も　わすれないようにね。
Don't forget a bucket of water, too.

| 火 | fire
[kun] ひ
[on] カ |  | | | | | |

| 火
fire, flame | 火曜日
Tuesday | 火星
Mars | 花火
fireworks | 火山
volcano | 火事
fire (destructive burning) |

| 光 | light, shine
[kun] ひかり／ひか－る
[on] コウ | | | | | | |

| 光
light | 光る
to shine | 日光
sunlight |

|  水 | water
[kun] みず
[on] スイ |  | | | | | |

| 水
water | 噴水
fountain | 水曜日
Wednesday | 水星
Mercury | 水泳
swimming |

<ruby>車<rt>しゃ</rt></ruby>りん Wheels (車・自)

<ruby>うば車<rt>ぐるま</rt></ruby>に、てお<ruby>し車<rt>ぐるま</rt></ruby>。
A baby carriage and a wheelbarrow.

<ruby>さんりん車<rt>しゃ</rt></ruby>に、<ruby>自<rt>じ</rt>てん車<rt>しゃ</rt></ruby>に、<ruby>いちりん車<rt>しゃ</rt></ruby>。
A tricycle, a bicycle, and a unicycle.

それから、<ruby>でん車<rt>しゃ</rt></ruby>に、<ruby>自<rt>じ</rt>どう車<rt>しゃ</rt></ruby>。
A train and a car!

ぜんぶ <ruby>車<rt>しゃ</rt></ruby>りんが ついてます。
All of them have wheels.

ぜんぶ <ruby>車<rt>くるま</rt></ruby>と いう じが ついてます。
All of them have the character *kuruma* (車).

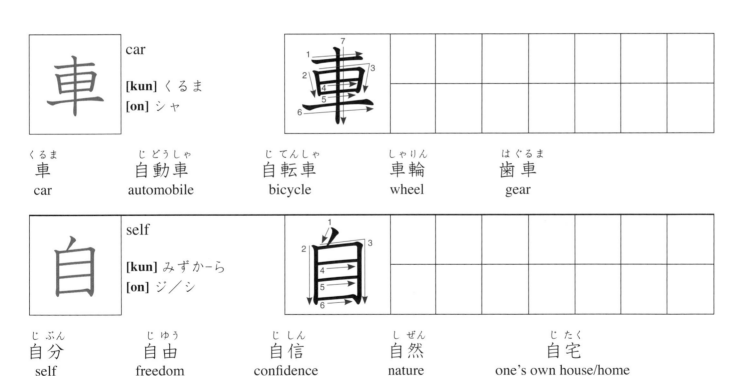

車
car
[kun] くるま
[on] シャ

| くるま
車
car | じどうしゃ
自動車
automobile | じてんしゃ
自転車
bicycle | しゃりん
車輪
wheel | はぐるま
歯車
gear |

自
self
[kun] みずから
[on] ジ／シ

| じぶん
自分
self | じゆう
自由
freedom | じしん
自信
confidence | しぜん
自然
nature | じたく
自宅
one's own house/home |

田んぼ Rice Fields (田・土・米)

三じかん　でん車に　のって、きたに　いくと、

いつのまにか　田んぼが　つづく。

If I take a train and go north for three hours, all I see are rice fields.

田んぼの　田の　じは　田んぼの　かたち。

The character 田 in 田んぼ (rice field) has the shape of a rice field.

田んぼで　お米を　つくります。

We make rice in a rice field.

はるの　田んぼは　土の　いろ。

Rice fields in the spring are the color of the soil.

なつの　田んぼは　みどりいろ。

Rice fields in the summer are green in color.

あきの　田んぼは　こがねいろ。

Rice fields in the fall are gold in color.

ふゆの　田んぼは　ゆきの　いろ。

Rice fields in the winter are the color of the snow.

田 rice field

[kun] た／だ
[on] デン

た
田んぼ
rice paddies

いなか
田舎
countryside

ゆでん
油田
oil field

やまだ
山田さん
Mr./Ms./Mrs. Yamada

土 soil, ground, earth

[kun] つち
[on] ド／ト

つち
土
soil

ねんど
粘土
clay

どようび
土曜日
Saturday

どせい
土星
Saturn

とち
土地
(piece of) land

米 rice

[kun] こめ
[on] マイ／ベイ

こめ
米
rice

げんまい
玄米
brown (unpolished) rice

はくまい
白米
white (polished) rice

べいこく
米国
U.S.A.

金メダル Gold Medal (金・銀)

一ばん　よく　できた人は
The person who did the best

金メダルを　もらいます。
receives the gold medal.

二ばん目に　よく　できた人は
The person who did the second best

銀メダルを　もらいます。
receives the silver medal.

三ばん目に　よく　できた人は
The person who did the third best

銅メダルを　もらいます。
receives the bronze medal.

いっしょうけんめい　やれば、
メダルを　もらえなくても、えらいです。
Even if you could not receive a medal,
you did a great job if you tried your best.

| 金 | gold, money, metal

[kun] かね
[on] キン | 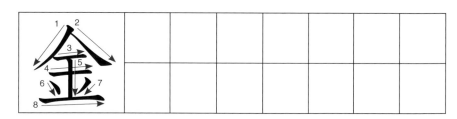 | | | |

金	金メダル	お金	金属	金曜日	金星
gold	gold medal	money	metal	Friday	Venus

| 銀 | silver

[kun] none
[on] ギン | | | | |

銀	銀メダル	銀色	銀行	銀河系
silver	silver medal	silver color	bank	the Milky Way galaxy

^{おお} ^{いぬ} ^{ちい} ^{いぬ}
大きい犬と、小さい犬
A Big Dog and a Small Dog (大・小・犬)

^{おお}　　　^{いぬ}
大きい　犬は　ゆっくり　あるきます。
A big dog walks slowly (with big steps).

^{ちい}　　　^{いぬ}
小さい　犬は　はやあしで　あるきます。
A small dog walks quickly (with many tiny steps).

^{おお}　　　^{いぬ}
大きい　犬は　ゆっくり　ワンと　ほえます。
A big dog barks slowly, "Wan".

^{ちい}　　^{いぬ}
小さい　犬は　はやくちで
キャン　キャンと　ほえます。
A small dog barks quickly, "Kyan Kyan".

| 大 | big, large, great

[kun] おお-きい
[on] ダイ／タイ |  | | | |

^{おお}
大きい
big　　　　^{だいがく}
大学
university　　　　^{おとな}
大人
adult　　　　^{たいせつ}
大切な
important

| 小 | small, little

[kun] ちい-さい／こ／お
[on] ショウ | | | | |

^{ちい}
小さい
small　　　　^{しょうがくせい}
小学生
elementary school student　　　　^{おがわ}
小川
a brook, a stream　　　　^{しょうせつ}
小説
novel

| 犬 | dog

[kun] いぬ
[on] ケン |  | | | |

^{いぬ}
犬
dog　　^{こいぬ}
子犬
puppy　　^{ばんけん}
番犬
watch dog　　^{のらいぬ}
野良犬
stray dog

21

かがみ Mirror (右・左・中)

右_{みぎ}てを　あげた。
I raised my right hand,

でも、かがみの　中_{なか}では　左_{ひだり}てが　あがった。
but my left hand rose in the mirror.

左目_{ひだりめ}で　ウインクした。
I winked with my left eye,

でも、かがみの　中_{なか}では　右目_{みぎめ}で　ウインク。
but my right eye winked in the mirror.

さかだちした。
I did a hand stand.

こんどは　かがみの　中_{なか}でも　さかだち。
This time, I was also doing a hand stand in the mirror.

どうして、はんたいに　なるのは　右_{みぎ}と、左_{ひだり}だけなんだろう？
I wonder, why do only right and left switch?

右　right

[kun] み ぎ
[on] ユウ／ウ

み ぎ
右
right

み ぎ き
右利き
right-handed person

う せつ
右折する
to turn right

左　left

[kun] ひ だ り
[on] サ

ひ だ り
左
left

さ せつ
左折する
to turn left

さ ゆう
左右
right and left

中　middle, inside

[kun] な か
[on] チュウ

な か
かばんの中
inside the bag

ちゅう がく せい
中学生
junior high school student

ちゅう しん
中心
center

ちゅう かん し けん
中間試験
mid-term exam

シーソー Seesaw (上・下・兄)

ギッタン　バッコン　ギッタン　バッコン
Gittan bakkon gittan bakkon

お兄ちゃんが　下がると、わたしが　上がる。
When my brother goes down, I go up.

わたしが　下がると、　お兄ちゃんが　上がる。
When I go down, my brother goes up.

上に　いって、下に　いって。
Going up, going down.

下に　いって、上に　いって。
Going down, going up.

ギッタン　バッコン　ギッタン　バッコン
Gittan bakkon gittan bakkon

above, on, up, superior

[kun] うえ／あ−がる／
のぼ−る／あ−げる

[on] ジョウ

うえ
テーブルの上
on the table

あ
上がる
to go up

じょうず
上手
skillful

のぼ　でんしゃ
上り電車
in-bound train

おくじょう
屋上
housetop, roof

---

under, down, inferior

[kun] した／さ−がる／
く だ−る／さ−げる

[on] カ／ゲ

した
テーブルの下
under the table

さ
下がる
to go down

へ た
下手
unskillful

くだ　でんしゃ
下り電車
out-bound train

ち か
地下
underground

げ た
下駄
Japanese wooden clogs

---

elder brother

[kun] あに／お−にい−さん

[on] ケイ／キョウ

あに
兄
one's elder brother

にい
お兄さん
elder brother

きょうだい
兄弟
siblings

男 の 子と、 女 の子 Boys and Girls (男・女・好)

男の子は　たいてい　おにごっこが　好き。
Boys usually like to play tag.

女の子は　たいてい　ままごとが　好き。
Girls usually like to play house.

でも、女の子も　ときどき　おにごっこを　します。
But sometimes, girls also play tag.

男の子も　ときどき　ままごとを　します。
Sometimes, boys also play house.

26

男

man, male

[kun] おとこ
[on] ダン／ナン

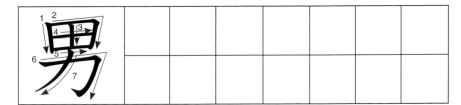

_{おとこ ひと}
男の人
man

_{おとこ こ}
男の子
boy

_{ちょうなん}
長男
eldest son

女

woman, female

[kun] おんな
[on] ジョ

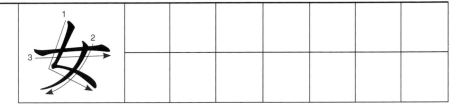

_{おんな ひと}
女の人
woman

_{おんな こ}
女の子
girl

_{かのじょ}
彼女
she

_{じょゆう}
女優
actress

好

love, like, favorite

[kun] すーきな／すーく
[on] コウ

_す
好きな
favorite

_{す きら}
好き嫌い
likes and dislikes

_{こう き しん}
好奇心
curiosity

字をつかって Using Letters (字・文・本・書)

あいうえおは　日本の字。
あ, い, う, え, and お are Japanese letters.

アメリカの字は　ABC。
American letters are A, B, and C.

字が　あるから、文が　書ける。
Because we have letters, we can write a sentence.

文を　つなげると、おはなしに　なる。
If we connect sentences, we can make a story.

おもしろいと、本にも　なる。
If it is interesting, it becomes a book.

わすれないうちに、おもったことを　書いておこう。
Before we forget, let's write down our thoughts.

字

letter, character

[kun] none
[on] ジ

じ
字
letter, character

かんじ
漢字
kanji (Chinese characters)

すうじ
数字
numbers

しゅうじ
習字
penmanship

文

sentence, literature

[kun] ふみ
[on] ブン／モン

ぶん
文
sentence

ぶんか
文化
culture

もじ
文字
character, letter

ぶんがく
文学
literature

本

origin, main, book

[kun] もと
[on] ホン

ほん
本
book

えほん
絵本
picture book

ほんとう
本当の
true, real

書

write, book, document

[kun] かーく
[on] ショ

か
書く
to write

しょどう
書道
calligraphy

きょうかしょ
教科書
textbook

学校 School (学・校)

めだかの学校は　川の中。
The fishes' school is in the river.

ありの学校は　土の中。
The ants' school is in the ground.

たこの学校は　うみの中。
The octopi's school is in the ocean.

くまの学校は　森の中。
The bears' school is in the forest.

ぼくの学校は　まちの中。
My school is in the town.

学　study

[kun] まな－ぶ
[on] ガク／ガッ

学ぶ
to learn

学生
student

学者
scholar

学習
learning

数学
mathematics

入学
admission into a school

校　school

[kun] none
[on] コウ

学校
school

校長
school principal

高校生
high school student

校舎
school building

校庭
school grounds

校門
school gate

校正
proofreading

私の先生 My Teacher (私・先・生)

わたし せんせい
私の先生は
My teacher

わたし
いつも 私の はなしを
よく きいてくれます。
always listens to what I say.

わたし
それから、いつも 私に
「がんばって」って、いってくれます。
She also always tells me, "Try your best!"

せんせい
先生、ありがとう。
Thank you, Teacher!

---

 private

[kun] わたし／わたくし
[on] シ

わたし 私	しどう 私道	しりつだいがく 私立大学
I	private road (path)	private university

---

 ahead, previous

[kun] さき
[on] セン

さき 先に	せんせい 先生	せんげつ 先月	せんしゅう 先週	せんぱい 先輩
on ahead	teacher	last month	last week	one's senior

---

 live, birth

[kun] いーきる／うーまれる
[on] セイ／ショウ

い 生きる	う 生まれる	いっしょう 一生	たんじょうび 誕生日	せいねんがっぴ 生年月日
to live	to be born	lifetime	birthday	date of birth

せいせいどうどう
正正堂堂 Acting Right, Playing Fair (四・年・正)

こうたくんは、小学校の 四年生。
Kōta is a 4th grader in elementary school.

正しいと おもったことは、正正堂堂と やります。
Whenever there's something that he thinks is right, he does it boldly.

だれかが まちがったことを していたら、
Whenever there is someone who is doing something wrong,

正正堂堂と ちゅういします。
he lets them know without hesitation.

じぶんが まちがっていたら、正正堂堂と あやまります。
Whenever he realizes that he is wrong, he apologizes valiantly.

やきゅうの しあいでは、正正堂堂と たたかいます。
Whenever he plays baseball, he competes fairly.

四 four

[kun]] よっ−つ／
よん／よ

[on] シ

よっ
四つ
four (things)

よ じ
四時
four o'clock

し がつよっか
四月四日
April 4th

し き
四季
four seasons

年 year, age

[kun] とし

[on] ネン

とし
年
year, age

とし よ
お年寄り
elderly people

よ ねんせい
四年生
fourth grade

きょねん
去年
last year

らいねん
来年
next year

正 correct, right

[kun] ただ−しい

[on] セイ／ショウ

ただ
正しい
correct, right

せいかく
正確な
accurate

しょうがつ
正月
the New Year

せい ぎ
正義
justice

しょうじき
正直な
honest

サッカーボール Soccer Ball (五・六・角・形)

サッカーボールは、五角形と、六角形で、できている。

A soccer ball is made of pentagons and hexagons.

五角形の　まわりには、六角形が　五つ　ある。

Each pentagon is surrounded by five hexagons.

六角形の　まわりには、六角形が　三つと、五角形が　三つ　ある。

Each hexagon is surrounded by three hexagons and three pentagons.

五角形と、六角形って、なかよしなんだな。

Pentagons and hexagons seem to get along very well.

ぴったり　くっついて、まんまるの　ボールを　つくってる。

They fit together perfectly to form a perfect ball!

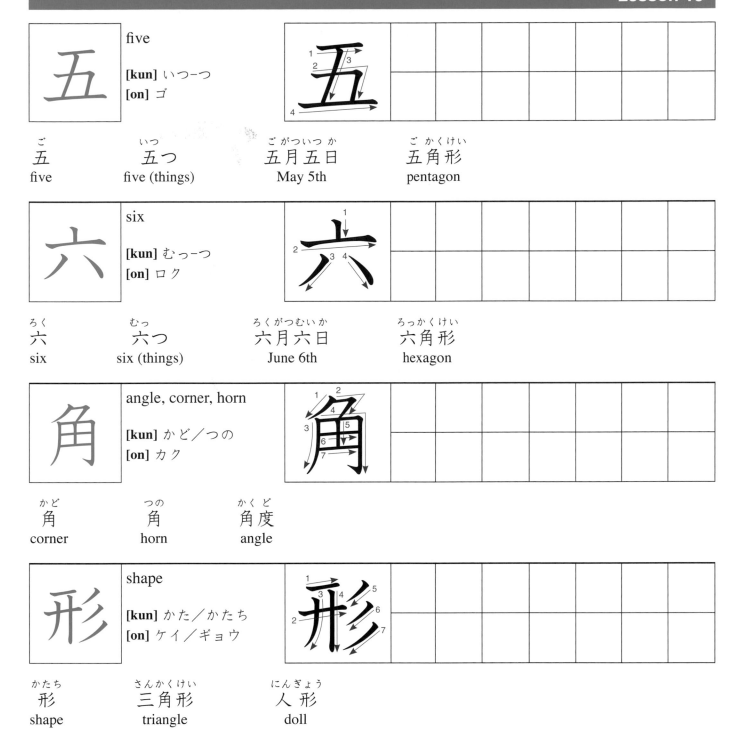

五 five

[kun] いつ-つ
[on] ゴ

ご
五
five

いつ
五つ
five (things)

ごがついつか
五月五日
May 5th

ごかくけい
五角形
pentagon

六 six

[kun] むっ-つ
[on] ロク

ろく
六
six

むっ
六つ
six (things)

ろくがつむいか
六月六日
June 6th

ろっかくけい
六角形
hexagon

角 angle, corner, horn

[kun] かど／つの
[on] カク

かど
角
corner

つの
角
horn

かくど
角度
angle

形 shape

[kun] かた／かたち
[on] ケイ／ギョウ

かたち
形
shape

さんかくけい
三角形
triangle

にんぎょう
人形
doll

インディアン・ボーイズ Indian Boys (七・八・九・十)

ひとり　ふたり　さんにん
一人、二人、三人の　インディアン
One little, two little, three little Indians

よんにん　ごにん　ろくにん
四人、五人、六人の　インディアン
Four little, five little, six little Indians

しちにん　はちにん　きゅうにん
七人、八人、九人の　インディアン
Seven little, eight little, nine little Indians

じゅうにん
十人の　インディアン・ボーイズ
Ten little Indian boys

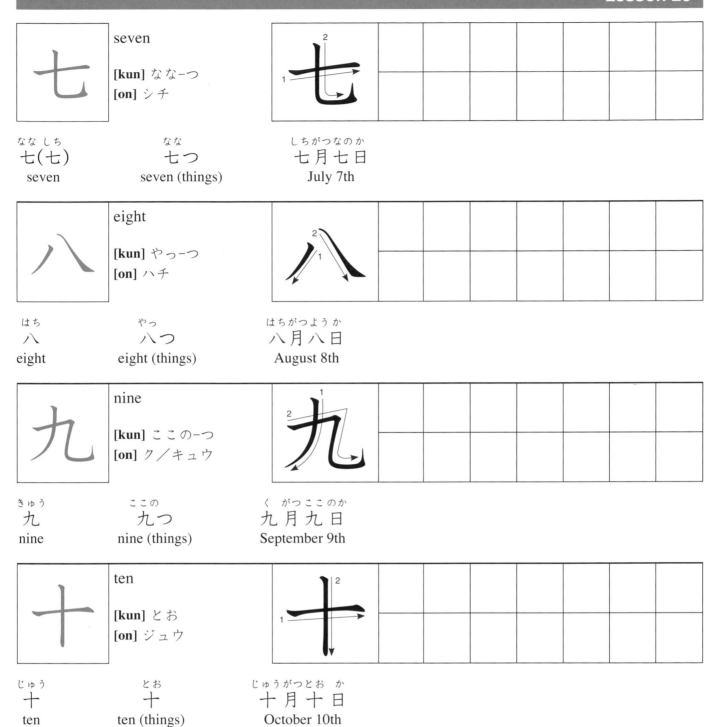

七
seven

[kun] なな–つ
[on] シチ

なな しち
七(七)
seven

なな
七つ
seven (things)

しちがつなのか
七月七日
July 7th

八
eight

[kun] やっ–つ
[on] ハチ

は ち
八
eight

やっ
八つ
eight (things)

はちがつようか
八月八日
August 8th

九
nine

[kun] ここの–つ
[on] ク／キュウ

きゅう
九
nine

ここの
九つ
nine (things)

く　がつここのか
九月九日
September 9th

十
ten

[kun] とお
[on] ジュウ

じゅう
十
ten

とお
十
ten (things)

じゅうがつとお か
十月十日
October 10th

おこづかい My Allowance (百・千・円・玉)

<ruby>百<rt>ひゃく</rt></ruby><ruby>円<rt>えん</rt></ruby><ruby>玉<rt>だま</rt></ruby>

おとうさんが 百円玉を 二<ruby><rt>ふた</rt></ruby>つ くれました。
My dad gave me two one-hundred-yen coins.

おばあちゃんは 百円玉を 三<ruby><rt>みっ</rt></ruby>つ くれました。
My grandma gave me three one-hundred-yen coins.

おじいちゃんは 五百円玉を 一<ruby><rt>ひと</rt></ruby>つ くれました。
My grandpa gave me one five-hundred-yen coin.

おこづかいが 千円<ruby><rt>せんえん</rt></ruby>に なりました。
My allowance totaled one thousand yen.

38

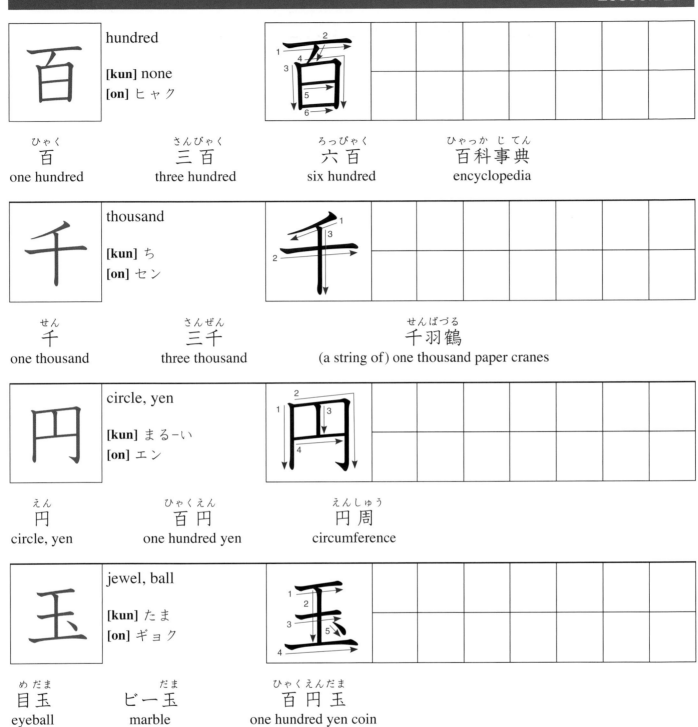

百
hundred
[kun] none
[on] ヒャク

ひゃく
百
one hundred

さんびゃく
三百
three hundred

ろっぴゃく
六百
six hundred

ひゃっか じ てん
百科事典
encyclopedia

千
thousand
[kun] ち
[on] セン

せん
千
one thousand

さんぜん
三千
three thousand

せんばづる
千羽鶴
(a string of) one thousand paper cranes

円
circle, yen
[kun] まる-い
[on] エン

えん
円
circle, yen

ひゃくえん
百円
one hundred yen

えんしゅう
円周
circumference

玉
jewel, ball
[kun] たま
[on] ギョク

め だま
目玉
eyeball

だま
ビー玉
marble

ひゃくえんだま
百円玉
one hundred yen coin

どうぶつ Animals (耳・足・手・長)

うさぎは　耳が　長いです。
Rabbits have long ears.

だから、小さい　おとも　よく　きこえるのかな。
I wonder if that's why they can hear tiny sounds.

だちょうは　足が　長いです。
Ostriches have long legs.

だから、とべないけど、はやく　はしれるのかな。
I wonder if that's why they cannot fly, but can run fast.

さるは　手が　長いです。
Monkeys have long arms.

だから、木から　木へと、どんどん　とびうつれるのかな。
I wonder if that's why they can leap from tree to tree.

でも、さるも　ときどき　木から　おちるんだって。
But I heard that monkeys sometimes fall from trees, too.

hand

[kun] て

[on] シュ

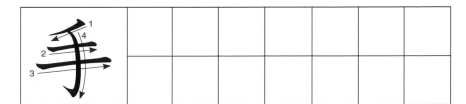

て
手
hand/arm

て がみ
手紙
letter

しゅじゅつ
手術
surgery

あくしゅ
握手する
to shake hands

foot, leg, pair, suffice

[kun] あし／た−りる／
た−す

[on] ソク

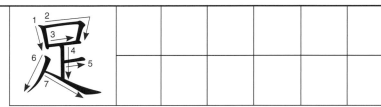

あし
足
foot/leg

えんそく
遠足
field trip

ふ そく
不足
lack

た
足りる
sufficient

ear

[kun] みみ

[on] ジ

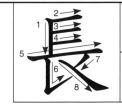

みみ
耳
ear

ちゅうじ
中耳
middle ear

じ び か
耳鼻科
ear and nose doctor

長

long, eldest, chief

[kun] なが−い

[on] チョウ

なが
長い
long

ちょうなん
長男
the eldest son

しゃちょう
社長
(company) president

せいちょう
成長
growth

41

ちから つか
力 を 使って Using My Strength (体・力・使)

ぼくは　まいにち　体を　きたえています。
I strengthen my body every day.

ごぜんちゅうは、
In the morning,

うでの　力を　使って、うでたてふせ。
I do pushups using the strength of my arm.

ごごは、
In the afternoon,

おなかの　力を　使って、ふっきん。
I do sit-ups using the strength of my stomach.

晩ご飯の　あとは、
After dinner,

ゆびの　力を　使って、パパと　ゆびずもう。
I do finger wrestling with my dad using the strength of my finger.

体

body

[kun] からだ
[on] タイ

からだ
体
body

たいりょく
体力
physical strength

たいいく
体育
physical education

たいそう
体操
gymnastics

力

strength, power, ability

[kun] ちから
[on] リョク／リキ

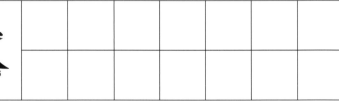

ちから
力
strength, power

どりょく
努力
effort

ぼうりょく
暴力
violence

きょうりょく
協力する
to cooperate

いんりょく
引力
gravity

すいりょくはつでんしょ
水力発電所
hydraulic power plant

使

use, servant

[kun] つかーう
[on] シ

つか
使う
to use

たいし
大使
ambassador

たいしかん
大使館
embassy

てんし
天使
angel

出る人と、入る人
People Who Exit and People Who Enter
(入・出・電)

でんしゃ
電車や、エレベーターでは、
In trains and elevators,

出る人が先、入る人は　あと。
the people who exit should go first,
and the people who enter should go after.

入る人が　先に　入ると、出る人は　出にくいから。
If people enter first, those who are exiting cannot exit easily.

出る人が　先に　出たら、入る人も　入りやすいから。
If people exit first, those who are entering can enter easily.

---

 enter, put in
[kun] はいーる／いーれる
[on] ニュウ

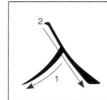

入る	入れる	入り口	入学する
to enter	to put in	entrance	to enter a school

---

 emerge, put out
[kun] でーる／だーす
[on] シュツ

出る	出す	出口	出発
to come out	to put out	exit	departure

電 electricity
[kun] none
[on] デン

電気	電力	電車	電話	停電
electricity, electric light	electric power	electric train	telephone	blackout, power failure

休むとき When Resting (立・休・強)

しまうまは よく 立ったまま 休みます。
Zebras often rest while standing.

てきが きたら、すぐ にげられます。
They can quickly run away if predators come.

ライオンは 強いので、
Lions are strong,

いつも よこになって 休みます。
so they often rest while lying down.

でも、ゆだんたいてき！
But relaxing too much could be your worst enemy!

立	stand, establish [kun] た-つ／た-てる [on] リツ							

立つ	私立大学	組み立てる	独立
to stand	private university	to assemble	independence

休	rest [kun] やす-む [on] キュウ	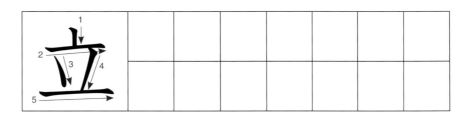						

休む	休み	休日	昼休み	夏休み
to rest, to be absent	break, holiday	holiday, day off	lunch break	summer vacation

強	strong, force [kun] つよ-い [on] キョウ	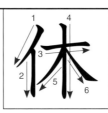						

強い	強制する	勉強する	強調する
strong	to enforce	to study	to emphasize

はた Flags（白・赤・青）

日本の　はたは、赤と、白。
The Japanese flag is red and white.

カナダの　はたも、赤と、白。
The Canadian flag is also red and white.

アメリカの　はたは、赤と、白と、青。
The American flag is red, white, and blue.

フランスの　はたも、赤と、白と、青。
The French flag is also red, white, and blue.

white, confess

[kun] しろ／しろ－い
[on] ハク

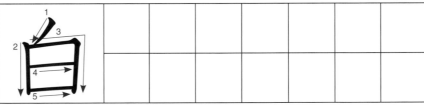

白	白い	白鳥	漂白	告白
white color	white	swan	bleach	confession

red

[kun] あか／あか－い
[on] セキ

赤	赤い	赤ちゃん	赤道
red color	red	baby	equator

blue

[kun] あお／あお－い
[on] セイ

青	青い	青空	青年	青信号
blue color	blue	blue sky	young man/people	green (traffic) light

貝の名前 The Names of Shellfish (貝・名・前・何)

この大きい　貝の　名前は　はまぐりです。
The name of this big shellfish is *Hamaguri*.

この小さい　貝の　名前は　あさりです。
The name of this small shellfish is *Asari*.

このうずまきの　貝の　名前は　さざえです。
The name of this spiral shellfish is *Sazae*.

このきれいな　貝の　名前は　何だろう？
I wonder, what is the name of this beautiful shellfish?

貝

shellfish

[kun] かい

[on] （バイ）

かい
貝
shellfish

かいがら
貝殻
shell

しんじゅがい
真珠貝
pearl oyster

名

name, famous, members

[kun] な

[on] メイ／ミョウ

なまえ
名前
name

ゆうめい
有名な
famous

めいし
名刺
business card

前

before, front, previous

[kun] まえ

[on] ゼン

まえ
前
before, front, previous

さんねんまえ
三年前
three years ago

ぜんはん
前半
the first half

何

what

[kun] なに／なん

[on] none

なに　　か
何を買いましたか。
What did you buy?

なん
これは何ですか。
What is this?

なんにん
何人ですか。
How many people?

はや
早おき Getting Up Early (早・朝)

早おきは　三文の　とく。
さんもん
The early bird catches the worm.

あさ　はや
朝、早く　しごとを　はじめると、
If you start your job early in the morning,

はや
しごとが　早く　おわります。
you can finish your job early.

はや
しごとが　早く　おわれば、
If you finish your job early,

ゆっくり　あそべます。
you can spend more time having fun.

あさ　はや　　　　　　　　　いちにちじゅう
だから、朝、早く　おきると、一日　中　きもちいいんです。
This is why I feel great all day when I wake up early in the morning.

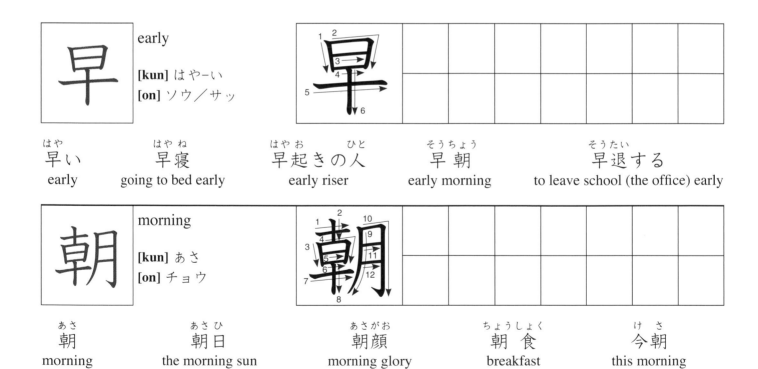

| 早 | early
[kun] はや‐い
[on] ソウ／サッ |

はや
早い
early   はやね
早寝
going to bed early   はやお　ひと
早起きの人
early riser   そうちょう
早朝
early morning   そうたい
早退する
to leave school (the office) early

| 朝 | morning
[kun] あさ
[on] チョウ |

あさ
朝
morning   あさひ
朝日
the morning sun   あさがお
朝顔
morning glory   ちょうしょく
朝食
breakfast   けさ
今朝
this morning

あさばん
朝晩
in the mornings and evenings

夕がたの空 The Sky at Dusk (夕・空・帰)

夕がたの　空は　赤いろ。
The sky at dusk is a red(dish) color.

お日さまが、しずんで、もえているから。
That's because the sun has set and is still burning.

夕やけ　こやけを　うたいながら　帰りましょう。
Let's go home while singing *Yuyake Koyake* (Evening Glow).

ああ、よかった。
Oh, I feel lucky.

帰るうちが　あるから。
I have a home to return to.

夕	evening [kun] ゆう [on] セキ

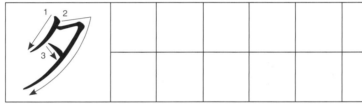

夕方	夕日	夕焼け	夕食	七夕
evening	the evening (sinking, setting) sun	evening glow	supper, dinner	the Star Festival

空	sky, air, empty, vacant [kun] そら／あ－く／ あ－ける／から [on] クウ

空	空気	空港	空席	空手
sky	air	airport	vacant seat	karate

帰	return [kun] かえ－る [on] キ

帰る	帰国する	帰国子女
to go/come back	to return to one's country	returnee student

春ののはら Spring Field (草・花・春)

春の　のはらを　ここちよく　してくれるのは
What makes the spring field a comfortable place

草と、花です。
is the grass and flowers.

草は、うすみどりの　じゅうたん。
The grass is a light green carpet.

花は、そのじゅうたんの　きれいな　もよう。
The flowers are the beautiful patterns on that carpet.

春の　のはらで　おひるねを　すると、
If I take a nap in the spring field,

そよかぜが　のどを　くすぐって、
the breeze tickles my throat,

やさしい　お日さまが　いいゆめを　見させてくれます。
and the nice sun helps me have a pleasant dream.

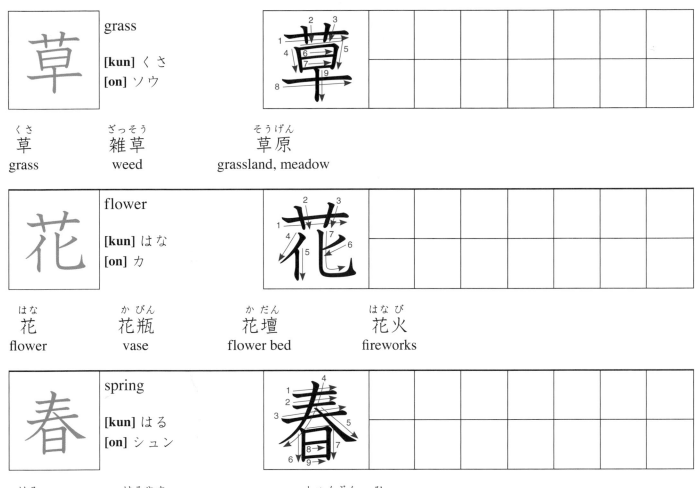

草
grass

[kun] く さ
[on] ソウ

く さ
草
grass

ざっそう
雑草
weed

そうげん
草原
grassland, meadow

花
flower

[kun] はな
[on] カ

はな
花
flower

か びん
花瓶
vase

か だん
花壇
flower bed

はな び
花火
fireworks

春
spring

[kun] はる
[on] シュン

はる
春
spring

はるやす
春休み
spring recess

しゅんぶん ひ
春分の日
the day of the vernal equinox

<ruby>竹<rt>たけ</rt></ruby> Bamboo (竹・馬・歩)

<ruby>空<rt>そら</rt></ruby>を　とぶ　<ruby>竹<rt>たけ</rt></ruby>は　<ruby>何<rt>なん</rt></ruby>ですか？

What is bamboo that can fly in the sky?

--<ruby>竹<rt>たけ</rt></ruby>とんぼです。

That's a take-tonbo (a flying toy made of bamboo).

のって　<ruby>歩<rt>ある</rt></ruby>ける　<ruby>竹<rt>たけ</rt></ruby>は　<ruby>何<rt>なん</rt></ruby>ですか？

What is bamboo that you can get on and walk with?

--<ruby>竹馬<rt>たけうま</rt></ruby>です。

That's a take-uma (Japanese stilts).

<ruby>竹<rt>たけ</rt></ruby>から　<ruby>生<rt>う</rt></ruby>まれた　<ruby>女<rt>おんな</rt></ruby>の<ruby>子<rt>こ</rt></ruby>は　だれですか？

Who is the girl who was born from bamboo?

--かぐやひめです。

That's Kaguya-hime (Princess Kaguya in an old Japanese story).

竹

bamboo

[kun] たけ
[on] チク

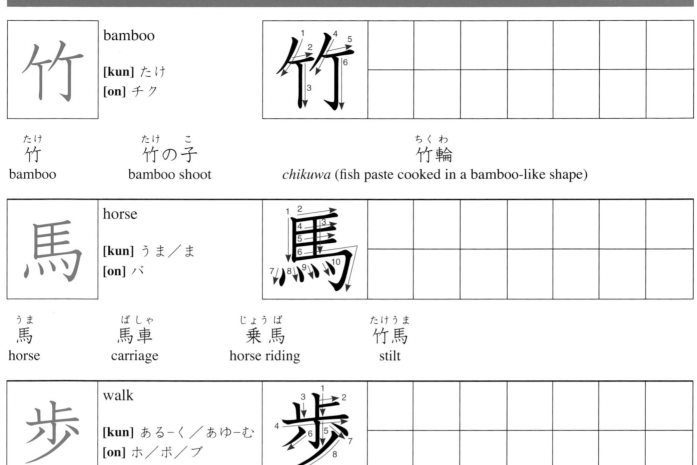

<u>たけ</u>
竹
bamboo

<u>たけ こ</u>
竹の子
bamboo shoot

<u>ちく わ</u>
竹輪
chikuwa (fish paste cooked in a bamboo-like shape)

馬

horse

[kun] うま／ま
[on] バ

<u>うま</u>
馬
horse

<u>ば しゃ</u>
馬車
carriage

<u>じょうば</u>
乗馬
horse riding

<u>たけうま</u>
竹馬
stilt

歩

walk

[kun] あるーく／あゆーむ
[on] ホ／ボ／ブ

<u>ある</u>
歩く
to walk

<u>さん ぽ</u>
散歩する
to take a walk

<u>ほ こうしゃ</u>
歩行者
pedestrian

虫の音楽会 Bugs' Concert (虫・音・夜)

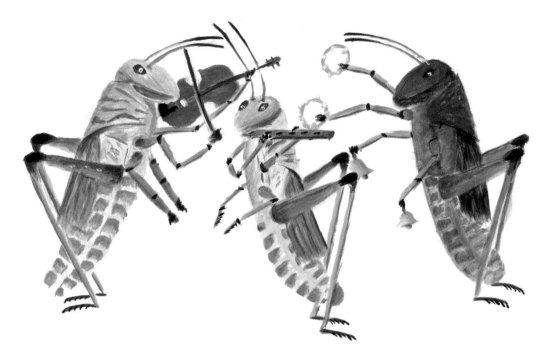

あきの　夜は　虫の　音楽会。
On autumn nights, there is a bugs' concert.

いろんな　音が　きこえます。
You can hear all sorts of sounds.

バイオリンみたいに
Like a violin,

キュッ　キュッ　キュッ　キュッ、キュッ　キュッ　キュッ。
Kyu kyu kyu kyu kyu kyu kyu

すずの音みたいに
Like little bells,

コロ　コロ　リン　リン、コロ　コロ　リン。
Koro koro rin rin koro koro rin.

ふえの音みたいに
Like a flute,

ピー　ピー　ヒョロロ　ピー　ヒョロロ。
Pī pī hyororo Pī hyororo

ぜんぶ　虫の　こえなんです。
They are all the voices of bugs.

54

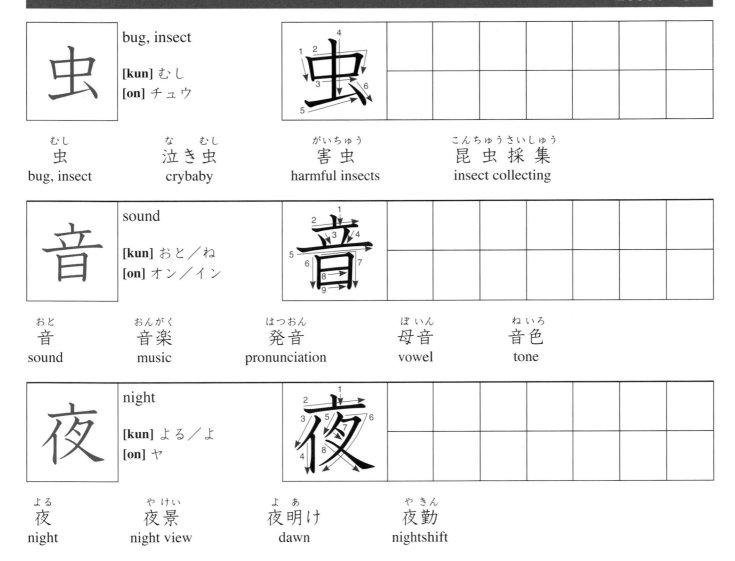

	bug, insect **[kun]** むし **[on]** チュウ	虫						

むし
虫
bug, insect

な　むし
泣き虫
crybaby

がいちゅう
害虫
harmful insects

こんちゅうさいしゅう
昆虫採集
insect collecting

	sound **[kun]** おと／ね **[on]** オン／イン	音						

おと
音
sound

おんがく
音楽
music

はつおん
発音
pronunciation

ぼいん
母音
vowel

ねいろ
音色
tone

	night **[kun]** よる／よ **[on]** ヤ	夜						

よる
夜
night

やけい
夜景
night view

よ　あ
夜明け
dawn

やきん
夜勤
nightshift

村^{むら}と、町^{まち} Villages and Towns (村・町・家・店)

一人^{ひとり}で　くらすと、さびしいです。
If I lived by myself, it would be lonely.

となりに　家^{いえ}が　ないと、さびしいです。
If there was no house next to mine, it would be lonely.

家^{いえ}が　いくつか　近^{ちか}くに　できると、村^{むら}が　できます。
If some houses were built around mine, we could make a village.

もっと　人^{ひと}が　きてくれると、町^{まち}が　できます。
If more people came, we could make a town.

学校^{がっこう}も、びょういんも、ちかくに　できると、もう　あんしん。
If we got a school and a hospital in the neighborhood, we would feel safe.

お店^{みせ}も、レストランも、できると、とても　にぎやか。
If we got stores and restaurants, it would be very lively.

ぼくの　町^{まち}は、にぎやかな　町^{まち}。
My town is a lively town.

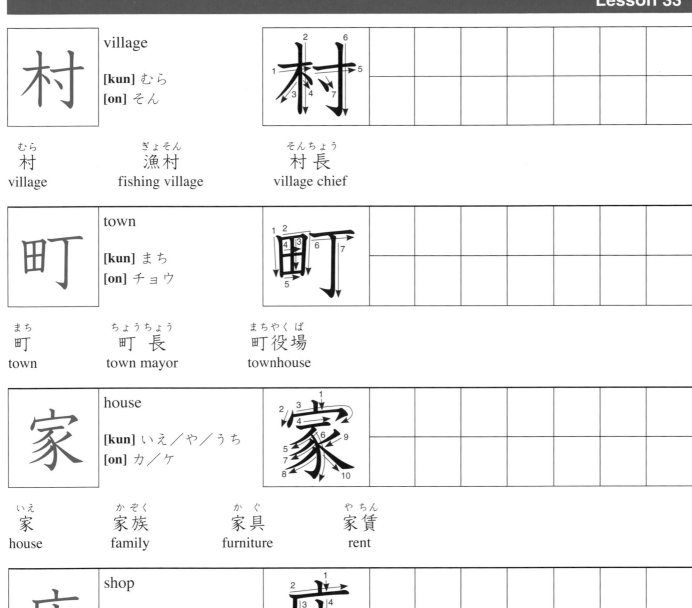

村
village
[kun] むら
[on] そん

むら
村
village

ぎょそん
漁村
fishing village

そんちょう
村長
village chief

町
town
[kun] まち
[on] チョウ

まち
町
town

ちょうちょう
町長
town mayor

まちやくば
町役場
townhouse

家
house
[kun] いえ／や／うち
[on] カ／ケ

いえ
家
house

かぞく
家族
family

かぐ
家具
furniture

やちん
家賃
rent

店
shop
[kun] みせ
[on] テン

みせ
店
shop

てんいん
店員
store clerk

しょてん
書店
bookstore

宝石 Gemstones (王・石・宝)

王さまは　宝石を　あつめるのが　大好きです。
Kings like to collect gemstones.

ダイヤモンド、　ルビー、　サファイアに、　エメラルド。
まだまだ、　たくさん　あります。
They have diamonds, rubies, sapphires, emeralds and so much more.

みんな　きれいに　光ってる。
They all shine beautifully.

キラキラ、　ピカピカ、　光ってる。
Kirakira, pikapika, shining.

でも、どれも　石の　なかまなんです。
But they all come from rocks.

かっこよく　きって、よく　みがくと、きれいに　なるんです。
Once you cut them nicely and polish them well, they become beautiful.

いい　名前が　あると、宝石って、よばれるんです。
If they have nice names, they can be called gemstones.

58

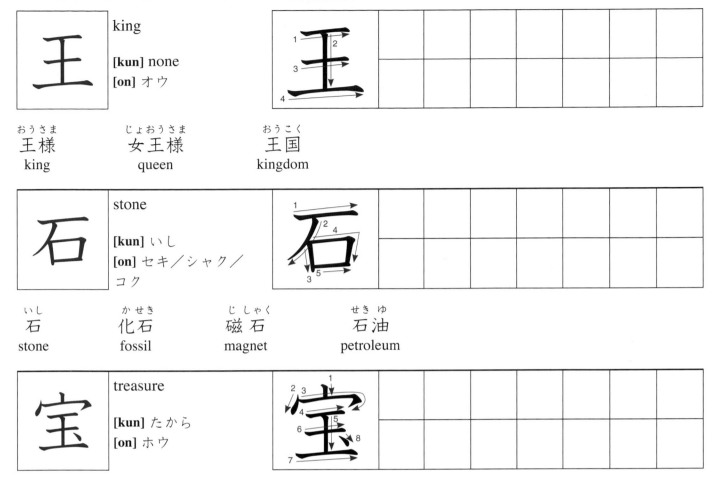

王　king

[kun] none
[on] オウ

おうさま
王様
king

じょおうさま
女王様
queen

おうこく
王国
kingdom

石　stone

[kun] いし
[on] セキ／シャク／
コク

いし
石
stone

かせき
化石
fossil

じしゃく
磁石
magnet

せきゆ
石油
petroleum

宝　treasure

[kun] たから
[on] ホウ

たから
宝
treasure

ほうせき
宝石
jewel, gemstone

こくほう
国宝
national treasure

糸 Threads (糸・毛・作)

毛糸は、ひつじの 毛で 作ります。
Woolen threads (yarn) are made of sheep's hair.

あったかい セーターが できます。
With yarn, we can make a warm sweater.

きぬの 糸は、かいこの まゆで 作ります。
Silk threads are made of silkworms' cocoons.

きれいな きものが できます。
With silk, we can make a beautiful kimono.

めんの 糸は、わたで 作ります。
Cotton threads are made of cotton plants.

きもちいい ティーシャツが できます。
With cotton, we can make a comfortable T-shirt.

くもの 糸は、くもが 自分で 作ります。
Spider threads are made by spiders themselves.

ほかの 糸とは ちがいます。
Their threads are different from other types of threads.

ほそくて、見えにくくて、虫が つい ひっかかって しまいます。
They are thin, hard to see, and bugs get trapped in them easily.

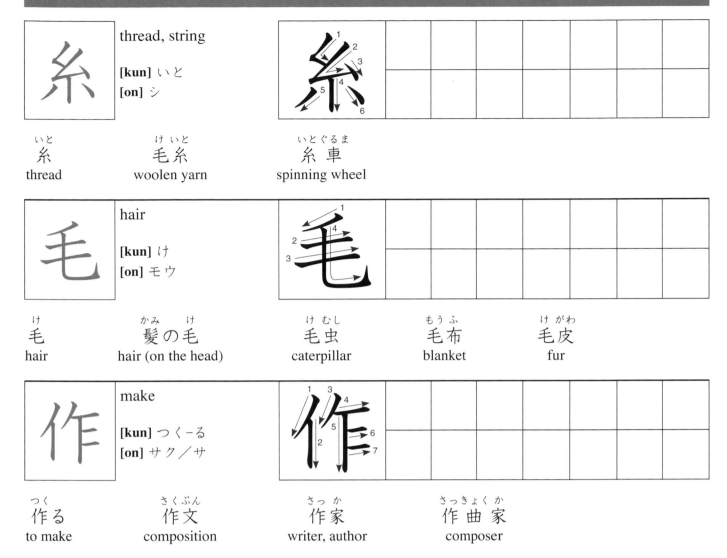

糸
thread, string
[kun] いと
[on] シ

いと
糸
thread

けいと
毛糸
woolen yarn

いとぐるま
糸車
spinning wheel

毛
hair
[kun] け
[on] モウ

け
毛
hair

かみ　け
髪の毛
hair (on the head)

けむし
毛虫
caterpillar

もうふ
毛布
blanket

けがわ
毛皮
fur

作
make
[kun] つくーる
[on] サク／サ

つく
作る
to make

さくぶん
作文
composition

さっか
作家
writer, author

さっきょくか
作曲家
composer

てるてるぼうず Teru-Teru Bozu (雨・天・気)

あしたは　えんそく。
We have a field trip tomorrow.

あめ
雨が　ふらないように、
To prevent it from raining,

つく
てるてるぼうずを　作って、うたいます。
I'll make a teru-teru bozu (shiny-shiny Buddhist priest), and sing.

♪ てるてるぼうず　てるぼうず
♪ Teru-teru bozu, teru bozu

てんき
あした　天気に　しておくれ。♪
Please make tomorrow a sunny day. ♪

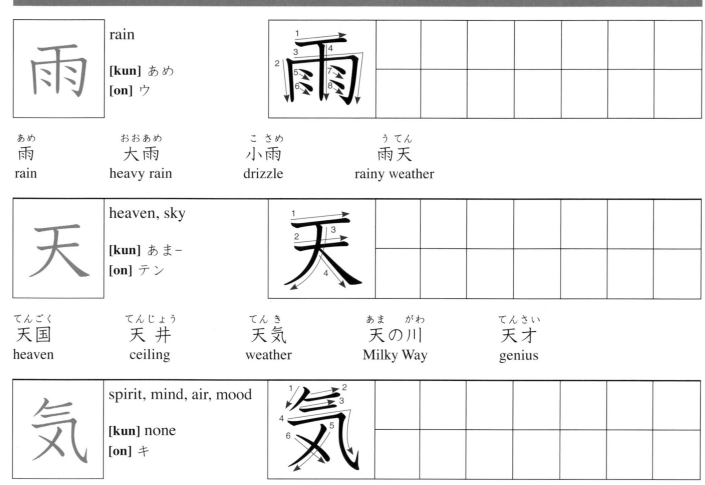

雨
rain
[kun] あめ
[on] ウ

あめ
雨
rain

おおあめ
大雨
heavy rain

こさめ
小雨
drizzle

うてん
雨天
rainy weather

天
heaven, sky
[kun] あまー
[on] テン

てんごく
天国
heaven

てんじょう
天井
ceiling

てんき
天気
weather

あま がわ
天の川
Milky Way

てんさい
天才
genius

気
spirit, mind, air, mood
[kun] none
[on] キ

げんき
元気な
healthy, fine

びょうき
病気
sickness

きも
気持ち
feelings

くうき
空気
air

にんき
人気
popularity

n'	wa	ra	ya	ma	ha	na	ta	sa	ka	a
ん	わ	ら	や	ま	は	な	た	さ	か	あ
		り ri		み mi	ひ hi	に ni	ち chi	し shi	き ki	い i
		る ru	ゆ yu	む mu	ふ fu	ぬ nu	つ tsu	す su	く ku	う u
		れ re		め me	へ he	ね ne	て te	せ se	け ke	え e
	を o	ろ ro	よ yo	も mo	ほ ho	の no	と to	そ so	こ ko	お o

n'	wa	ra	ya	ma	ha	na	ta	sa	ka	a
ン	ワ	ラ	ヤ	マ	ハ	ナ	タ	サ	カ	ア
		リ ri		ミ mi	ヒ hi	ニ ni	チ chi	シ shi	キ ki	イ i
		ル ru	ユ yu	ム mu	フ fu	ヌ nu	ツ tsu	ス su	ク ku	ウ u
		レ re		メ me	ヘ he	ネ ne	テ te	セ se	ケ ke	エ e
	ヲ o	ロ ro	ヨ yo	モ mo	ホ ho	ノ no	ト to	ソ so	コ ko	オ o